I Lift Up My Heart

I Lift Up My Heart

A Book of Christian Poetry
By Deborah DR Kralich

Copyright 2015
Published by Ruskras Corner
The United States of America

All rights reserved. no part of this book may be reproduced, stored in a retrievable program, or transmitted by any means, electronic or mechanical, including photocopying, recording, or otherwise as may be expressly permitted by the full copyright statute or in writing by the author.
ISBN 978-1942542094
TX0008204032

Cover Art by Deborah D Russo
This is a work of poetry and art containing constructed personae. Any resemblance to actual persons, living or dead, incidents, situations, events, places and locations, past or present, are purely coincidental.
God is real.

Introduction

I was working on my next mystery,
(Also I do write fictional history.)
When slam! from out of nowhere
Poetry issued this dare,
Aggressively jumping the queue,
Pushing prose behind,
Demanding next spot in the line.
I admit I did dig in old files.
But most of this is brand new.
I expected an experience restrictive.
But words to my screen fairly flew.
I found verse is addictive.
Unexpected surprise, but it's true.
This poem that fact does prove.
Next, the cover I drew.
I toyed with the images for a while,
Trying to capture His smile.
Trying to better depict it.
Then He hinted sublime-
I consider this project through.
You're neglecting all the chores you should do.
Finish! For this, you've no more time.
So along with my art to observe,
As my testimonial victory
I humbly offer my words,
My phrases, and my rhymes,
Hoping His cause they all serve.

Contents

Introduction- 3
List of Poetry- 4,5
Dedication- 6
Daily Prayer- 7
Affirmation Song- 8,9
So Much More Perfect Than Mine- 10
The Fabric of My Mind- 11
Perfect Transmitter- 12
His Voice in a Thousand- 13
I Lift up My Heart- 14
Favors- 15
Through Dark Forests- 16
In Cold Dark- 17
Warm, Strong, and Unafraid- 18
Follow the Leader- 19
Day Job- 20,21
Behind the Second Chance- 22,23
Try Reading the Instruction Manual- 24
Recruited- 25
Prayer for the Enemy at the Door- 26
Never Alone- 27
Hackers- 28,29
Our Real Enemies- 30
Betrayal Encounter- 31
Student Success- 32
So Long to All of You People- 33

Identified- 34

Contents

Supervised- 35
Crashing Doubts- 36,37
Review Process- 38
Know Me- 39
You Have Me- 40
Wedding Prayer- 41
Throughout the Ages- 42.43
History Lesson- 44
The Night Crowd- 45
Longing for Days of Old- 46,47
The Great Writer- 48
So I Did Not Do Anything…49
Special Assignment- 50
Accepted At Last- 51
The Source- 52
Cleansing- 53
Faith be My Companion- 54
Sensations- 55
Daydreaming- 56
Appendix Pages- 57
About the Author- 58
About the Cover Art- 59
Letter To the Editor and Publisher- 60
FAQ About the Author's Other Works- 61
To the Reader- 62
Finale- 63

Dedication

First to the One who made me
And saved me.
As I hope my books will attest,
I get editorial support from the Best.
He does not stand on convention,
Constantly refreshing my efforts anew.
I'm aided also by a crew
He provided for me with good intentions.
So my family gets Honorable Mentions-
Johanna, Carl, Joseph,
And Thomas, too.

Daily Prayer

Oh, Lord, I pray
Take care of all of us today.
Oh, Lord, I pray
Take care of all travelers by night and day.
Oh, Lord, I pray
Watch my house when I am at home or away.
Oh, Lord, I pray
Take care of all those who have to work for pay.
Oh, Lord, I pray
Take care of all who serve in the midst of the fray.
Oh, Lord, I pray
Watch over my church, keep all her enemies at bay.
Oh, Lord, I pray
Send us healing, let there be no wreaths we lay.
Oh, Lord, I pray
Watch over the animals, both pet and stray.
Oh, Lord, I pray
Let You my works justly portray.
Oh, Lord, I pray
Take care of all of us today.
Oh, Lord, I pray.

Affirmation Song

YES! THERE IS A CHRIST!- HE IS ALIVE!

AND ALL THE REST IS NONSENSE.

STOP WHAT YOUR DOING, CONFESS.

THINK OF THE CONSEQUENCES.

DON'T SETTLE FOR ANY LESS.

YES! THERE IS A CHRIST!- HE IS ALIVE!

MORE THAN THE IMPLICATION

THAT WE'LL LIVE FOREVER,

THERE IS AN EXPLANATION-

HE WILL FORSAKE US NEVER.

YES! THERE IS A CHRIST!- HE IS ALIVE!

TODAY WE SEE SO LITTLE,

A QUICK LOOK INSUFFICIENT.

WE ARE CAUGHT IN THE MIDDLE

OF A WORLD SO DEFICIENT.

YES! THERE IS A CHRIST!- HE IS ALIVE!

HIS LIGHT SHOWS US HIS WAY.

RESURRECTION ENTICES.

NOW WE GLIMPSE THE GREAT DAY

WE LEAVE THIS WORLD'S DEVICES.

THERE WE WILL BEHOLD HIM

THEN HIS LIGHT ENFOLDS US.

YES! THERE IS A CHRIST!- HE IS ALIVE!!

So Much More Perfect than Mine

I love You for every thought You have given me.
I love You for every Word You have spoken.
For You are the rhapsody of my soul,
The instrument of my life.
I send my love to You as best I can.
Embers through haziness.
My love for you is like a genuine stone
Amidst broken jewels.
Seen only in the lack of shadows,
Dimming in artificial light.

You love me for nothing.
You love me even though
I am one of millions who strive.
One of many besides.
Yet You send Your love like a beacon
Penetrating dense rock.
Your love for me is a flawless gem
Emanating from perfect life.
A fiery sparkle like ice
Seen in the darkest light.

Light of the stars,
You have reached out Your hand through all time,
Reached out Your heart,
Sent Your love,
Your infinite love
So much more perfect than mine.

The Fabric of My Mind

You are the very fire of my existence.
You wove the fabric of my mind.
You planted the soul within me.
You formed everything I am.
From You I derive
The very courage upon which I walk.
I am nothing without You.
You are my Everything.
I exist, today, because of You.

Perfect Transmitter

As imperfect transmitter as I am,
Send love through me.
For whatever I have to give
Is an expression of Your love to others,
Which enables me to receive Your
Love through them.
And therefore that is how I am loved,
How we all are loved.
So enrich my life with love
Hard as it may be.
So that I might fully receive
All the love You have for me.

His Voice in a Thousand

I could recognize His voice in a thousand.
No sound is more dear.
His voice is amazingly gentle.
It calms my chaotic mind
Like nothing else ever could.
He says-
Everything is fine.
I am here.
I love you.

I Lift Up My Heart

I lift up my heart
As the scriptures say.
As He reaches to take,
The crust of sin falls apart
And flakes away.
Yet a little remains
Where my fingers still hold.
I fear letting go so much.
Despite the stain,
I need the organ to live,
To pump blood through my veins,
And keep death at bay.
Yet I will continue to partake
And on the journey embark
Until the day He proclaims-
Let loose, be bold!
All you must give!
Relinquish your touch
And all flaws will depart.
It is time to awake
To My promise of old.
Eternal joy now to start.

Favors

Evergreen is Thy love
When ours with seasons waiver.
You are there for all
Through darkness and strife.
Yet when we heed Your call,
We claim we are doing You a favor.
Perhaps when to us befall
Endless cold night,
Endless hard labor,
We will look up above,
Petition blessings to fall
And Thy grace to save us.

Through Dark Forests

Oh, Light in my darkness
Stray never from me.
Draw a wide mark lest
I fall from the path.
Off trails in the forest
So perilous and vast.
For my long journey
Equipment vital I seek.
Not gear, horse or harness,
I list here all I need-
Sight, first and last,
Christ Jesus to see.

In Cold Dark

Thy light is comfort to me.
In shadows of fear,
Thy voice, the only sound,
They face all I see.
The earth grows cold
And bitter clouds appear.
Thy arms keep me warm.
And Thy Word which I hear
Banishes threats that surround.
And all dangers that be.
My heart Thou does hold.
Thy hands shield me from harm.
Penetrating comfort is near.
Perfect protection I have found,
Making winter disappear.

Warm, Strong, and Unafraid

You who are cold with foreboding,
Be warm.
For God has your future.
If life around is imploding,
Be strong.
For Christ is here present.
If you fear solitude exploding,
Be unafraid.
For the Spirit blankets the earth in love.

Follow the Leader

Don't follow the crowd,
No matter which way they go.
They drown, never stand.
Be not diverted by their flow.
Only Christ can lead.
His directions are loud.
The path He does decree.
You cannot miss His command.
Read his Word and know.
Avoid chaos and harm.
He gathers His from the sea,
Safe from the storm,
Onto the land.

Day Job

I know not why the Lord gave me this type of life,
This job to do.
Whatever He had in mind, I haven't a clue.
And He was so specific that He wanted me here,
Doing these tasks of frivolous cheer.
I am sure that is true.
He could have made me useful more
In so many other ways.
But to me this is the lot in life He gave.
I could have been wealthy and born much fruit,
Giving much to the poor.
I could have saved sinners, endured strife,
Comforted the sick,
Enlightened the world, gone door to door.
But for the bills to pay
And meet my family's needs day by day
This is the pursuit
He sent to me,
Seeming to emphasize that life is curious that way.
And when I am reminded that for my sin
The price He did pay,
I feel so guilty when my trade
Seems like nothing but play.
So I confessed to Him-

Lord, I enjoy this easy wage,
I celebrate life too much every day.
Send me to live in poverty among those in need,
Among those in chains not free,
To witness in dens the devil made.
Or impose heartache and pain to see
So I may show the world I pray.
And in still voice, He replied-
I want you here, doing exactly what you do, just as I say.
When I said 'Follow Me',
It was to keep you from all that you suggest.
You are my child. I love you. I know what's best.
And if that's not convincing, recall I hold the big stick.
It's My choice.
I get to pick.
I choose which of your sails to trim.
I planned your existence.
I want you to live fully and in joy hear My voice.
And I didn't die for you to suffer, I rose to hear you rejoice.
Your potential is only reached with patience, persistence.
That is your test.
And always remember My sacrifice, My gift to you,
Includes peace and rest.
I am the Savior. I would never lead you astray.
I gave you this work, this life, because I knew how you
would serve Me best.
And that you would be happiest this way.

Behind the Second Chance
(A romance dedicated to writers of ETWG)

Christ was her first love.
Though she did not know it.
She deduced the comfort in the night
Came from fantasies of flight.
Thoughts of God did not fit.
In her arms she wanted a man,
Wedding dress, veil, and gloves,
Not some ethereal spirit
Unattainable above,
Coming with no party or band
Or excitement of lyrics.
She did not understand
That to have one, she needed two.
She thought the future was at hand
When she saw turtle doves.
Coming years secure in sight.
But the birds failed to coo.
And it all ended with fights.
Then she turned to Christ,
Her real first love and Light.
But she knew not what to do,
At functions meant for two.
Home alone would now she sit?

Then the Lord bade her, *Don't hide,*
Believe in My command.
To Me, first be true.
Build not your life on the sand,
But stoke the fire that I lit.
Find a church and commit.
This was all in My plan.
Follow My every cue
And all will soon be bright.
Now this was more than just a clue.
The first congregation she did scan.
And at once she knew.
For all it took was a glance.
There he sat in a pew.
And her second love flew
Right back to her side.
Now she could love him right.
Knowing that the First Love
Stands behind the second chance.

Try Reading the Instruction Manual

Religion we did flaunt
Still we felt the world pass us by
So we were compelled to sigh,
List our wants denied.
And question without fear-
First, why are You so shy?
We never see You here.
Why do You run and hide?
We need You to appear.
Next, Lord, tell us what You want.
Conflicting rules do taunt.
Third, we need specific whys-
And we went on and on
Until He interrupted at the ninth.
At His answer we felt cheer.
Just His attention was a high.
Though His reply was a slight jibe-
***M**ust be some fault with y'alls ears.*
My commands are loud and clear.
And blindness does you haunt.
For I am in plain sight
In all that you hold dear.
Say prayers day and night.
If doubts this does not daunt,
There is a manual I did write.
Passed down through years,
***B**ible- guide to life.*

Recruited

Proud of my skill.
Willing to serve.
In faith I feel strong.
He smiles at my youth
And sends me a curve.
Stripped of all talents.
Lacking the means to fulfill.
Confused at the truth,
Searching for balance,
I love Him still.
My wait is long.
He keeps me in reserve,
Sending grace in advance,
His plan to reveal
A life of joy all along
In doing His will.

Prayer for the Enemy at the Door

I do not fear,
Not much.
I do realize
I must not compromise.
I do not tremble
At the doorbell I hear.
Yet suddenly I hide
At the sound on my ear.
For I know the lies,
The words that surprise
And no way resemble
The truth I hold dear.
Decent people otherwise,
They cannot see with my eyes
They are too near.
So stories they devise
To explain me as such.
Solving puzzles with a quick alibi
So veracity disappears.
If I pull the door wide,
The danger is clear.
Lord, be my crutch,
I verbally appeal.
Don't let them get inside.
Be my shield and their guide.
Send them far away from here.

Never Alone

After conscious decision to roam,
I was lost in the dead zone.
Bankrupt, evicted from home.
Nothing left over to sign.

Seeing I was enslaved and in line
For clothing haphazardly sewn
And meager pickings on bones,

Christ led me to find
Pieces of life left behind,
A way to stand on my own.
I could never had done it alone.

Christ cut the ropes that did bind
My arms to the columns of stone.
Dispelling all I had known.
Harmonizing discordant tones.

Christ shattered the lights that did blind
My eyes to the limits of the mind
And the price of the spirit disowned.

Like petals from a flower unwind
And to the wind are now all blown,
Christ healed the past for all time.
No more debt, He did pay mine in kind.

Hackers

You disprove all accusations hurled.
So we are perplexed.
We know you mind works oddly.
So we find new ways to demean.
We know you can't be Godly.
No suffering prearranged.
So you should be entertained
By computer game
Or play or song or sex.
Like all the young expect.
But you write and draw and paint,
Old fashioned and quaint.
Not caring if you are seen.
So we slipped into your past.
And this is what we gleaned.
You were always strange,
Living in your own world,
Happy when you shouldn't have been,
Ignoring social respect,
Aloof in the extreme.
Nothing about you is correct.
You don't fit the mold.
Now, we don't believe in saints.
So secret meetings we convene
To declare you be deranged,
And should justice intervene
And our efforts reject,
We will stage the scene.
You've no defense against our scheme.

I Lift Up My Heart

Deborah DR Kralich

To bolster my defense,
Much about all of you could be told.
No justice your minds hold.
When the facts come out in whole,
The world will not be sold.
And a true profile I can get.
You don't own the internet.
I will defend my name.
Silence no longer my game.
You may believe I've grown bold.
But I'm just doing what I am told.
I'm not seeking fame.
Just a little respect.
And to do His will of old.
If you don't like that aspect
You all can go be hanged.
I will live my dreams.
With me you can't connect.
I am a fighter, behold,
With equipment you can't see.
Don't claim victory just yet.
I don't easily fold.
I may have been attacked.
But you all have been hacked.
Evil flashes on your screens.
My monitor is still green.
I will turn my back,
Your memory will turn to black.
God will wipe you clean,
Leaving my hard drive intact.

Our Real Enemies

Don't fear entertainment.
It's just temporary noise.
Don't fear gaiety and laughter,
Lack of dignity and poise.
Fear war and estrangement,
Persecution and capture,
The strike of the sword,
And jealousy toward
Our joy in the rain.
For our enemies are not singers,
Artists, or chapters
In ephemera that profanes.
But far-off killers and captors
Who would see us all slain.
Plus those near that point fingers,
And at our faith, protest annoyed.
When we speak of our rapture,
They invoke the spectre of Freud
To imprison our joy.

Betrayal Encounter

It is now too late to ruin my life.
There's not that much of it left.
Thanks for your tries in the past.
I am much stronger as a result.
All that unnecessary strife,
All those patronizing lies,
That you never considered insults.
You thought you would save me from myself.
You knew not your efforts as such
Came straight from the gates of hell.
When on that time you do dwell,
And think how you stripped me unmasked,
I know you pat yourself on the back,
Thinking how wise you were my secrets to tell.
Yet I bet you do wonder why
Gushing gratitude to you I lack.
And why I don't keep in touch.
You thought you were just trying to help.
But you were used by the devil himself
To snare me innocent into his clutch
And place me into his cells.
You thought my fate had been cast
But Christ negated your spell.
For that I love Him so much.
Grateful to be beyond your false touch,
I took on the work He compelled.
If you have curiosity for my tasks,
Imagining a sad life too long having last,
Feeling good and smug about yourself,
Thinking in a superior world you have dwelt.
Brace your mind, for I have lived well.
My life is happy, productive and vast.
In His peace and light I have basked.
I have only wonderful stories to tell.

Student Success

No one in class is brighter.
You pass all tests with ease.
If you were only not a writer,
Think what you could achieve.
If you could change from poet,
If you just would do the math,
You'd attract the high and mightier
To direct a silvered path.
Success would flow, we know it.
Life's trials would be lighter.
To science you would owe it.
And in your fame, we'd bask.

I glimpse the brass ring flightier
So enticing and easy to grasp.
But I cannot do as you ask.
A titillating web you do weave.
Yet a beckoning bids me to leave.
I've transferred to a chosen class
That only the Master can teach,
There art I'm allowed to conceive.
And my soul I'm permitted to keep.
The strength of the Cross I clasp.
Your lure is far too weak.
His hold on me is tighter
Than efficacy could ever be.

Empiricists, hold no torch for me.
I can't submit to your intrigue.
I've a different height to reach.
Let me declare it in your speak-
He created me in His lab,
I'm designed just for my task.
He knew what I would need,
Programmed me to believe.
So I'll let my words fly higher.
I've only Him to please.

So Long to All of You People

Secrets of the mind,
Contentments of the heart
Lead my voice to incline,
Respectfully impart,
His words to my kind.
But they say, Don't start.
We believe not what you define.
Society's left Him behind.
The culture's course we chart.
For the pious we've no time.
You must have an ax to grind.
Do not be that sort.

My world profoundly jarred,
Their stinging words like darts.
In rejection I now find
I must cut the ties that bind,
And from them I must part.

Identified

When so much time goes by and I hear not a word,
What am I supposed to do?
I cannot go to the world.
I'm already judged cause of You.

Most unexpectedly,
Most unexpectedly,
You are there again so very near,
Speaking to me just as before,
Instructions loud and clear.

At what you say, I'm taken aback.
For the request is such a shock.
They'll know I'd never do that!
On my own, never give it a thought.

Lord, You command and I'll try to accede
To pay someone's way as You ask,
Repent my sin of greed.
Yes indeed,
I know it's You for a fact.

So now they will see me as cracked.
Yet, I'll stand up and cheer.
As heeding this request is sure
To brand me as Yours at last.

Supervised

They cannot say I'm crazy
And proclaim the Covenant New.
Now, I know it might be possible
That both of those are true.
Though I be a little hazy
On details and the rules,
I heard His call- *Obey Me!*
And it's seriously improbable
That I could be so fooled.
They're just being lazy
When they discount my point of view.
To them I say- Let my faith be.
I do not declare impossible
The way He came to you.
He gave me a different tool
To navigate the maze- He
Understood and knew
My mind was bound with glue.
I was just incapable
Of blind faith like the pious few.
It took lightning to amaze me
And cause me to see-
Time to quit stargazing
And set my telescope on truth.
So skepticism does not faze me.
His power is unstoppable.
The vision is not only dazing,
His Word follows through.
Directing all I say and do.

Crashing Doubts

Billions in the world.
More than ever before.
So how does God keep score?
Masses in the past,
Civilizations which swirled,
Now all in the clasp
Of the death at our door.
My mind is aghast.
Doubts rise up and roar.
Is our fate cast?
Are we dust to the core?
Can the spirit unfurl
Through a universe so vast
Its concept is lore?
How can faith last
Faced with such math?

Stars and sunlight twirl.
Reassurance is flashed.
From the heavens His words hurl.
Divine mysteries outpour
Pure and clear from the flask.
The universe is more
Than matter and gas.
Gates that are pearled
Are within your grasp.
And paradise in store
For My people unmasked.
Hearing this, my mind whirls.
His words show the path,
A sign that holds fast,
Sending my heart to soar,
And causing all my doubts to crash.

Review Process

*Know that I am God.
You put your faith before Me
Like playing cards on a table.
I have found your hand lacking.
No matter.
I will make up the defects Myself.*

Know Me

Know that I am Christ.
I reach out My hand to you.
And if you cannot reach far enough
I will extend My reach
Until yours and My fingers touch.
What weighs on your heart,
Weighs on Mine, also.

You Have Me

They may have wealth, acceptance, prestige.
They may have success, influence and ease.
They seem to never fail, never have flaws.
Friends gather round to render applause.
When you feel bereft and gaze towards these
Ignore what they have. You may be alone,
Struggling to follow all on your own,
Be not jealous, instead bend your knees.
For you are the richer. Look on them with glee.
You have much more. You have Me.

Wedding Prayer

Help us to love.
Permit us to always be together
And never let us be far from love.
Or separated from You.
For we do love You so.
And if our love for each other should waiver
Fill in the gaps with Your love.
If time or trial parts us,
Don't ever let us be alone.
Let us never be without love.
By the joy of Your grace
Let us never know any existence again
Without love,
Without God.

I Lift Up My Heart   Deborah DR Kralich

Throughout the Ages

From antiquity to state-of-the-art,
Faith in God
Leads to faith in oneself.
Those who trust only in culture
And believe the religions of science
Attract those who are vultures
And persons in compliance,
Joining crowds lost in the fog.
No more than a wheel's cog.
Promoting anarchy and violence
Until elites achieve new alliances.

Then revival prevails, faithful leap inside
The old rumbling cart
Of praising the Lord.
New bandwagons flash beside
And most jump aboard,
Following the Christian march.
Culture and science
Restricted to their rightful parts.

Listening to Christ
Sets the people apart.
The Nation does arise.
The church power attains.
But when individuals proclaim
The truths in their hearts
Each is met with disdain.

Personal faith is an art.
Keep it quiet to yourself.
We don't want to hear.
You might share it for gain.
You may not be what you appear.
We dare not risk
One like you on our list.
You are not our choice
So you cannot hear His voice.

I Lift Up My Heart
Deborah DR Kralich

We are now the crowd.
You must follow us.
Dare not question or complain
You might turn to dust.
On our horse leap astride,
Or we can make you depart.

All see them in power.
Others step aside,
Bowing to the robe and the tower.
Their message is loud.
Culture and science appear to bow.
Secularism falsely cowers.
Its deference belies
Its patience in disguise.

And when masses defiant
Reject rules the cathedral imparts,
It withdraws, dry and crisp
Behind a façade reliant.
Practicality does arise
And a blending does start
Pushing Him to the side.
And the cycle restarts.

Clouds of misery, want and fear
Accumulate worldwide.
Defeat and despair shower.
Even as society does complain,
Banishing religion back to the shelf,
Christ is present, still the same
With we who contain
Love for Him within our hearts.
Continuously our personal Savior reigns,
The pendulum swing He disdains,
Every eon is His hour.
Individually he does us claim
Saving one at a time, each unique self.

History Lesson

Jesus on a sunny morning
Is like Jesus on the darkest night.
Jesus on fine occasions
Is like Jesus at a vicious fight.
Jesus in prosperity and peace
Is like Jesus at the broken battle.
Observe the peril of our nation,
Now rejecting Him at its height,
Where words are caught in endless coining
And our world in perpetual fazing,
Our existence in a constant rattle
Jarring cultural implications.
Society oblivious to its plight,
Obsessed with consternation
That we who do believe
Still have content and soothing flight.
Our happiness belies just how much we need
His presence every time, everywhere, every site.
There is no lift, no joy, no joining
Of the heart and mind without His light.
See the past for those deviations
That cast a shadow left and right,
Imprinting misery so dazing.
Whole peoples left to bleed,
Led to slaughter like cattle
Over efforts to appease.
Understand the implication.
Those rejecting divine lead
Never had a chance to succeed,
Yielding humanity's greatest fatigue.
To escape that situation,
Summon we must His dazzling sight.
By which our enemies will see defeat.
And perish by His might.

The Night Crowd

Approaching in darkening film,
Offering a rosebud tight.
Join our crowd, they say.
Don't try to find your own way.
We will steer you right.
Just keep us in your sight.
And don't go quoting Him.
We reject that whim.
Join the masses that fight
Those myths of celestial flight.
We see your minds are slim.
You're inclined to run away.
We cannot make you stay.
Yet. You will all conform someday.

Christian soldiers, contemplate-
Once just culture's rim,
Now this eve they dominate
With growing range of hate.
World lanterns dim.
The nation tempting fate.
With power at its height,
It turns from joy to blight.
And freedom now is trimmed.
Glorious past condemned.
To reject the new outright
Is perilous in the night.
So before they rule the day,
America, make a play
To cut the bud from stem.
Flowers only bloom in Light.
Reject their slippery ways
Before the noose is tight.

Longing for the Days of Old

My talents did more suit
To a different time.
Why wasn't I placed
When I could bear more fruit?
With a chance to win the race?
Before the click of shutter
The prestigious drew the face.
In ages genteel, sublime,
When few could more than mutter,
Or letters only trace,
Commanders of words were royally recruited.
Prose and poetry placed
Authors top of the line.
Now at the bottom, disgraced,
My talents are maligned.
This period is moot,
Valuing guns, not butter,
The experience of pursuit.
Nothing here but clutter,
Lacking reason and the rhyme.
Not a semblance of the truth
All society does is flutter,
Culture falling more and more behind.
Fooled by the devil's ruse.
What justice in this era can I ever find?
I long for days of lace
When I could have been an ace.

I Lift Up My Heart

Deborah DR Kralich

I frame that scene outlined,
Vision clear in my mind.
At this picture window, I brood,
Griping to the One who wrote my fate,
My reflections less than kind.
Then He slams shut the blinds.
He conveys thoughts that are less than subtle,
Answering sharply mine-
To complain you are inclined.
Think before you whine.
You're here by My grace
And you are doing fine.
If I had let you loose
In golden eras you define,
You could have known the gutter.
You might not have made a dime,
Nor lived past age of nine.
Or maybe took to crime
Yielding the hangman's noose.
So, accept your place.
Stop all this rebuttal
And get back on line.
You need to pick up the pace.
Work will brighten up your mood
Your next book will soon be due.
And I expect follow through
On unfinished art you partially drew.
So He has ruled my case.
I'm privileged to serve in this time and space
Til the clock silences its chimes.

The Great Writer

God, the author of life,
He wrote us well,
Equipped for all strife.
Pointed the way,
It was ours to choose.
We went astray.
Defeat ran rife.
And we could not pay
Or bridge the distance fell.
In the darkest of night
Christ caught the knife,
Our horrors to quell,
And restore the Light.

So I Did Not Do Anything…

Awakened by thunder,
A flash of white.
Surrounded by clouds.
A jolt of the current,
Restoration by Light.
Prayers yielded healing
In the dark of the night.
Later will I wonder,
Asking out loud,
A question while kneeling,
Perhaps just a little proud,
Why me, why my plight?
What did I do to warrant
The joy of Thy sight?
Nothing of importance,
Came the reply,
Simple, blunt and not at all shy.
Yet I caught the truth on the sly.
With talent I may ponder.
And words confess my feelings,
Still alone I had no chance.
For at the cross, yielding,
Christ fought the fight.

Special Assignment

Place me where Thy will.
I endeavor to stay.
Work me as Thy want.
I strive to obey.
What else can I say?
He bathes me with love.
I can sing His praise
As all do above.
Yet I am here.
He wants something else.
He may like my song.
But He follows my day
And lingers near
Making me question myself.
Am I doing wrong?
I wonder and wander in a daze
Until He takes me in hand,
And says- *Do not welch.*
Don't sing with the band.
Find your own way.
Do Me justice yourself.
Honor Me as only you can.

Accepted at Last

Accepted at last.
Rejected no more.
A crowd at my feet.
Flowers at my door.
Yet what would fans say
If they all could see
A clandestine way
To learn all about me?
All the flaws of my past.
All my lacking now.
There is One who knows all,
Yet would stand by my side
When all that yell wow,
If they saw me before
Would be gone with the tide.
Swept fast from the shore.

The Source

The joy You bring
Yields the story I tell,
Which mirrors Your love,
Sparks me to sing
A song like a bell.
A fit like a glove,
Embraced by wings.
Holy Spirit cling,
Envelope me well
In the love of the King.

Cleansing

Dropped from the heart.
Spilled from the side.
Blood of the Lamb,
A great ocean tide
Sweeping the earth
In a flood that revives.
Sail me away
Through second birth
To another life.
With Him to abide.

Faith Be My Companion

Faith be my companion.
Stay close to my heart.
Courage be my inflexion
When my world falls apart.
No more opinions,
Subjection departs,
When the great expansion
Begins to start,
I'll dwell in His dominion
Never from Him to part.

Sensations

Unique is the flavor
Of His love. I savor
Sweet aroma all around,
Song in every sound,
The white cloud of healing,
Enthrallment upon kneeling.
Recipient of His grace,
Joy to see His face.

Daydreaming

Lift me away on Your fingertips.
I only desire You.
Touch me with charges of lightning.
Taking me higher, too.
I desire to rise and slip
Over the top and through
The mist via angel flight wings
To join the celestial few.
But if the time is not due,
The line a long hard queue,
My stint will post on the next clip.
I'll wait til You give me the cue.
Until then my heart can only sing
Of the day my dream will come true!

Appendix Pages

About the Author

It is obvious she is odd.
She writes poetry about God.
We suspect she's not after fame.
She's playing some other game.
She's at a stage few artists arrive at.
She considers her personal life private.
If to Christianity she wasn't inclined,
She'd probably live a life of crime.
Her portrait is not on her book.
She must be hiding her look.
Curiosity is unproductive and moot.
Go ahead and assume she is cute.
Her discipline is instrumental.
But she can be quite temperamental.
If you get a little inquisitive,
She might say mind your own business.
She may not ooze syrup or honey,
But her works are well worth the money.
Her books do not lack spice and sage,
So you will keep turning the page.

About the Cover Art

You cannot view Him
Like we do, they say.
Not being who you are
And living in your day.
Who are you to draw
The One without flaw?
Yes, my poor efforts fail.
Of course it cannot be right.
No one can paint Him,
Though many have tried.
Others sincere, had their work hailed,
Though they did no better,
My efforts they condemn.
Your work is too dim.
You use too much light.
Image doesn't conform to the letter.
You go against our rules.
And recall He suffered and cried.
How can you make Him smile
After all of His trial?
Recall His death was so cruel.
His face should hold tears,
As we masters have shown Him for years.
They are correct as they judge.
I understand the limits of the craft.
It is no likeness, I agree.
I don't hold a grudge.
But what would they say.
If I could paint what I truly see-
When the Resurrected Christ stands with me?
For then with joy He does laugh.

Letter to the Editor and Publisher,

If I cannot use adjectives and adverbs
I cannot fully say
How wonderful He is,
Nor describe the way
He fills me with bliss
When with poetry I pray.
If my words you do curb,
I cannot best describe
Nor fully tell His story.
For I need in my prose works
To subtly show His glory,
Not every redemption quickly spied.
So I refuse to strike
All the color in the skies,
All the ways the ocean lies,
All the sparkle in the eyes,
All the joys in the whys.
You may call me disturbed.
But I'm planning to preserve
All words ending in L Y.
And I don't think I can lose
Using all the nouns I choose,
Conveying clues by hook or crook,
Detailing every look.
If my style you don't like,
Wanting to publish just bland books.
Don't send me your invite.
The stubborn path I may hike.
His praise I still will write .

FAQ About the Author's Other Works

Why'd you pick that genre?
It's definitely the wrong one.
Why don't you appreciate
The value of foundation
In books that we create?
Your books of exclamation
Contain no information
That religion can relate.
They just cause more temptation
And may lead to your damnation.
Why shouldn't they be banned?

I have an explanation.
I offered cooperation
To write wording He dictates.
Trying to paraphrase salvation,
You won't perceive the entendré.
But He had a different plan.
The Bible holds His inspiration
And needs no additions to inflate,
Perfectly outlining where He stands.
It's all right if simplification
Helps others achieve appreciation.
But that genre spikes with sharp vibrations
Bursting faithful bookstands.
In works of the imagination
Christ has few sheep on hand.
And exists a plethora of demand.
So there I write at His instigation,
Trying to control my mystery creations
and not let the characters seize domination.
When I slip, He forgives, understands,
Knowing I try to keep his commands.

To the Reader

Thank you for reading this book
Would you please kindly write a review?
Find a booklover's den
And post your opinion therein.
I give thanks before you begin.
I hope you'll also take a look
At other works I have penned.
He also bids me write them.
I hope my poetry has not been too obscure.
I know sometimes I was demure.
If you find some are too dim,
Just skip those that stories recount.
Read only the praise
That describes how His love ascends.
I tried to keep it all about Him.
But I needed a higher word count
So the book wasn't lacking a page.
A minimum number of poems I had to accrue.
So He permitted me to draw a maze
And adopt personae in a few.
Therefore, a little hyperbole can be found.
Imagination unbound.
Plots creeping in with the sage.
And even that would not do.
So some of myself also slipped in.
This I simply could not prevent.
Yet of my lines, I would contend
Behind every word is His truth.
It matters not which poems have added hue.
What's important is that He loves you.

Finale

Shadows and lightning.
A thrill in the rain.
Treasures and secrets
On the desert plain.
Over flies the night wings.
Sky and mountain attain.
Whispering, discreet,
Blanketing moonbeams
With angel's refrain-
The King is coming!
You don't wait in vain.

www.ingramcontent.com/pod-product-compliance
Lightning Source LLC
Chambersburg PA
CBHW060721030426
42337CB00017B/2959